AT HOME AND ABROAD
WITH

DAKSA AND ARUN

Two Hindu children
visit India

STEVE HARRISON

M

Macmillan Education

To Justine

The events in this book are a kaleidoscope of the type of experiences enjoyed by children from Britain visiting their parents' place of origin. The events depicted herein are based on true experiences, though some are fictitious, and some of the characters have assumed names.

Acknowledgements

The author and publishers wish to thank and acknowledge the following people for their help in the preparation of this book.

Mr & Mrs C Ghariwala, Ish Taylor, Iswarbhai Patel and family, Baroda, Charu Ainscough, Bharat and Seema Lakdawala, Surat, Shirley Parkinson, P Parmar, Indian High Commission, Haksmuth Patel, Jyotika Patel, Jerambhai Patel, Yashwantri Mehta, Dipak Mehta and the Hindu Communities in Leicester and Preston.

They also wish to acknowledge the following photograph sources:

Caroline Penn p 17
Peter Larsen p 14
UNICEF photos p 15 – Bernard P. Wolff p 18, Satyan p 19, Jack Ling p 31, Abigail Heyman p 34, Sean Sprague p 35, T. S. Nagarajan p 38
World Bank photos pp 26, 39, 47 – Ray Wittin pp 15, 18, Harmit Singh p 35, Jaime Martin-Escobal p 39

All the remaining photographs were taken by Steve Harrison.

The publishers have made every effort to trace copyright holders, but where they have failed to do so they will be pleased to make the necessary arrangements at the first opportunity.

First published 1986

Published by
MACMILLAN EDUCATION LTD
Houndmills, Basingstoke, Hampshire RG21 2XS
and London
Companies and representatives
throughout the world

Printed in Hong Kong

ISBN 0 333 38609 4

CONTENTS

The Patel family   4

Leaving India   6

A new start   8

The Patels at home   10

Arriving in Bombay   12

The railway station   14

On the train   16

Baroda   18

Pradip's house   22

Navaratri   24

The wedding   28

Caste   30

Village life   32

Dassehra   40

Varanasi   42

Diwali   46

Teacher's notes   48

THE PATEL FAMILY

Daksa Patel is thirteen years old and her brother, Arun, is ten. Both were born in England. Their parents have lived in Britain for nineteen years. Before that they lived in India. Narendra Patel, the children's father, worked hard when he first came to live in Britain and saved as much money as he could. Soon after Daksa was born he bought a corner shop with his savings. The family have lived there ever since.

All the family speak English. This is the language the children use at school. Daksa attends the local high school and Arun is at primary school. The family also speak English in the shop, although with Indian customers they often speak in Hindi or Gujarati. When the shop is closed they move into their living-room and speak to each other in Gujarati.

Daksa and Arun's father was born in a small village in western India, in the state of Gujarat. Everyone in the village worked on the land. Narendra's family were landowners. The name Patel means 'farmer', and many people with the name are descended from farming families. As a young boy Narendra was taught all there is to know about farming. He expected to work on the farm all his life.

But times were changing in India. Water supplies to the land improved and new fertilisers were available. At the same time new machinery was being used by farmers. These machines could do the work which people had done before. This meant that although farmers were growing more and more crops, fewer workers were needed on the land.

Daksa and Arun Patel.

The tractor Daksa's grandad bought could do the work of ten men. ▶

One of the most important crops grown in Gujarat is cotton.
▼

After being picked the cotton is taken to the co-operative cotton press where it is baled and loaded onto lorries.
▼

LEAVING INDIA

Narendra was one of three sons who worked on the family farm. Old Mr Patel, his father, decided there was not enough work for himself and his three sons, so he sent his eldest son, Pradip, to the city of Baroda. This city has a good college and the young man trained as an engineer. When he left college he began work as a construction engineer in Baroda.

Mr Patel soon realised that he needed only one son to help him on the farm. He decided that one of his younger sons should go to Britain. At that time many young people from Gujarat were starting new lives in Britain. There was plenty of work there and more workers were needed. People willing to work hard could become successful. The people of Gujarat have always been willing to travel in order to find work. There are Gujaratis throughout East Africa and Asia. Many of the Gujaratis now in Britain came from East African states. Gujaratis have settled in many other parts of the world too.

Mr Patel decided that his middle son, Ish, should stay with him on the farm and his youngest son, Narendra, go to England with his wife. Mr Patel wrote to some Gujarati friends who had already settled in Britain and asked if they could help find work for Narendra. The friends wrote back to say that Narendra and his wife could stay with them in Leicester. They would help him find a job once he arrived.

This map shows from which part of India the Gujaratis come.

▼

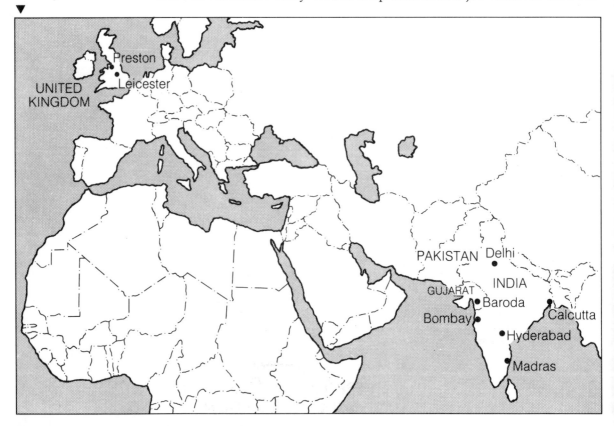

Mr Patel bought two single airline tickets from Bombay to London for his son and daughter-in-law. He wished the young couple good luck and said goodbye. He hoped to see them again one day, perhaps when they had children of their own.

Things to do

1 Gujaratis have moved from their home land to many parts of India. They have also settled in countries around the world. Find out when Gujaratis moved to East Africa (Kenya, Tanzania, Uganda and Zimbabwe) and South Africa. What jobs do they have in Africa?
2 Many Gujarati men have moved to the Arabian Gulf in the past few years. What industry has attracted them to the Gulf?
3 Most of the countries where Gujaratis live are English-speaking. Can you find out why countries so far apart use the English language?

Narendra and his wife stayed with their friends in this Leicester street.

A NEW START

Narendra found a job in a factory two weeks after arriving in Leicester. He did shift work and earned good money. The young couple lived with friends for two years until they had saved enough money to buy a small house of their own. Four years later Daksa was born. Narendra and his wife decided that they would like to own a small shop. Narendra asked friends and relatives to let him know of any businesses that he might buy.

He received a phone call from a Gujarati family in Preston. They were selling their small shop and had heard that Narendra was looking for one. The following Sunday Narendra drove up to Preston and agreed to buy the shop. Many Gujaratis move between towns such as Leicester, London, Bolton and Preston. Once a family has made a first move, other moves are easier. There are large Gujarati communities in all these towns and the groups keep in contact.

Narendra Patel could already speak English when he moved to the shop. He had learned it working in the factory. His wife could not speak English. She had not had a job and most of her friends were Gujarati women. She realised that if she was going to work in a shop then she must learn English. She joined an English class for adults where she learned very quickly.

▲
Narendra and his wife moved to Preston to open a shop. They sell groceries, cigarettes and drinks.

Every morning Mrs Patel helps the delivery man carry in the fresh bread.   ▶

A corner of the living-room is used as a shrine. A flame always burns in the shrine.

Mrs Patel prays at the shrine three times a day. As she prays she rings a small bell.

The Patels wanted their children to be British. They also wanted them to be able to speak Gujarati, so when Daksa and Arun were small their parents spoke to them in Gujarati. We all learn to speak by listening to people around us. Both the children soon learned to talk in their mother-tongue. But Narendra insisted that when the children reached the age of two they should begin to speak English. Many of the friends they played with in the street spoke English. By the time they started school Daksa and Arun could speak Gujarati and English.

Discussion point
When Narendra arrived in Leicester it took him only two weeks to find a job. In those days Britain needed workers in factories, hospitals and transport. Imagine you are a young Indian arriving in Britain today. Would you find a job as quickly as Narendra? Who might help you to find work?

9

THE PATELS AT HOME

The Patel family are Hindus. Hindus are not supposed to eat beef as cows are regarded as sacred and because Hindus have a great respect for life many avoid eating all meat, fish and eggs. Many Hindus also avoid drinking alcohol. Mrs Patel is vegetarian and does not drink alcohol. Narendra Patel sometimes eats chicken and occasionally drinks whisky or wine.

Arun visits the temple every week. He prays to Krishna.

Hinduism

Hinduism is one of the world's oldest religions. Some people have difficulty understanding Hinduism because there are so many gods. In fact, for most Hindus, all these images of the gods are different ways of seeing the one god. Hindus believe that God, the Supreme Soul, is present in everything and everybody. They also believe that each person has a soul which is born again and again, each time in a different body. In each life, you are punished or rewarded for what you have done in past lives, so whether you are born as a king or a beggar depends on how you behaved in a former life.

God shows himself to people in many ways. Many Hindus worship Vishnu, the Preserver, who comes to Earth from time to time to fight evil and protect us all. When Vishnu comes to Earth he appears as different people at different times. Two of his most popular appearances have been as the gods Krishna and Rama.

Many other gods and goddesses are worshipped by Hindus. Shiva, the destroyer, Ganesh, the remover of obstacles, Durga, the mother goddess, and Lakshmi, the goddess of wealth, all have their followers. All the gods have a story associated with them.

In the Patel house there is a room used only for prayer. There is a glass cabinet containing statues and pictures of many gods. The Patels visit the Hindu temple every week. There they pray, sing religious songs called bhajans and talk to other Gujaratis who live in the town. On some Sundays weddings are held at the temple.

The Patels were looking forward to the wedding of a friend in Bolton. When Mrs Patel told Daksa there was yet another wedding happening soon, Daksa asked where it would be.

DAKSA   Where will it be this time? Leicester? London?

MRS PATEL No. Baroda.

DAKSA   What? Baroda?

MRS PATEL Yes, Baroda. Your cousin Amita is going to be married. Your dad and I have decided to send you to India for the wedding. All our relatives keep asking to see you. This is a good time to visit.

DAKSA I can't believe it. Baroda! Does Arun know? I'll have to tell him.

Arun was not sure he wanted to go to India. He thought it would be dirty and full of starving people. Many people think this way about India. Perhaps it is because they only see pictures of India when there has been a disaster, such as a flood or famine.

▲
Ganesh is a very popular god. He helps people in times of difficulties.

All the gods have their own special story. Hindu ▶ parents teach their children about them.

11

ARRIVING IN BOMBAY

The children flew from London to Bombay on a jumbo jet. They felt strange as the plane soared into the sky. In England their lifestyle is a mixture of two cultures. They speak English and their house, television, furniture and most of their clothes are like those of their white friends. But the language they speak at home, their religion, and some of their food and clothes are Indian. They had no idea how they would get on in India. For the first time in their lives they were alone.

As they stepped from the plane the hot Indian air blew on their faces. It was like standing in front of an open oven. They felt very small and helpless as they stood in Bombay Airport. Daksa began to wonder if it had been such a good idea. She did not like the idea of being thousands of kilometres away from Britain.

She did not worry about being far from home for long. Someone was stealing their bags! 'Hey you, leave those bags alone. They belong to me,' Daksa called out.

The man who had picked up the cases turned round. He had a smile on his face. 'Yes, I know they are yours, young lady,' he said. 'Let me introduce myself. I am your father's brother — Uncle Pradip.' Daksa went red with embarassment. Arun simply laughed and laughed. Pradip was not upset. He agreed that he did not look much like the photographs he had sent. In fact, he was quite proud of the way Daksa had acted when she thought a stranger had taken her bags.

Pradip and the children travelled into Bombay by taxi. Arun was amazed to see Leyland double-decker buses and cars driving on the

▲
The children were surprised to see red Leyland double-decker buses in Bombay. In India they drive on the left as in Britain.

India has many magnificent palaces, museums, temples and forts. Tourists come from all over the world to see them. ▶

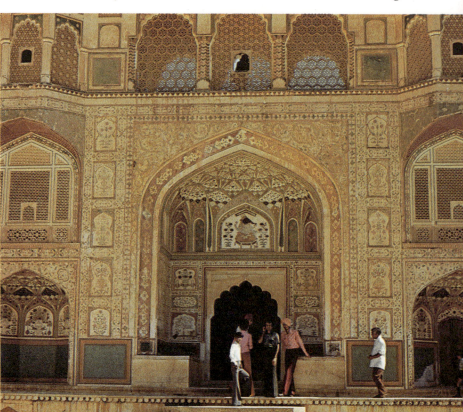

Tourists love to see snake charmers. You can see them in Bombay.

left as they do at home in Britain. Even the latest James Bond film was showing at the movies. Pradip told Arun not to be surprised. 'Bombay is like no other Indian city. It's very international. Business people from all over the world come here. Many Arabs come to hire workers for their own countries. Tourists from all over India and the world come to Bombay.'

They drove past many modern large hotels. There were old buildings built by the British when India was part of the British Empire. They saw snake charmers, fortune tellers and dancing monkeys. They were all there to entertain the tourists.

These elephants carry tourists.

THE RAILWAY STATION

Pradip took the children to a large restaurant. Daksa was surprised when her uncle ordered chicken and a glass of beer for himself.

DAKSA   Uncle, Mum told me Hindus in India are very strict. She said they don't eat meat or drink alcohol.

PRADIP   When I lived in the village I was a strict vegetarian and I didn't drink any alcohol. Now I've changed. I travel a great deal on business and I enjoy a drink now and then. When I get back to Baroda I can't have any alcohol. You see Baroda is in the state of Gujarat. It is against the law for anyone to drink alcohol in Gujarat. Here in Bombay it's allowed. We call this a wet state. Gujarat is a dry state.

DAKSA   You're like my dad. He only started to eat meat and drink alcohol when he moved to the city.

The three of them arrived at the railway station for the 01.00 train from Bombay to Ahmadabad. They would travel as far as Baroda.

Indian railway stations are incredible places. In some there are electric, diesel and steam trains. The stations are busy twenty-four hours a day. Sometimes you see whole families on the platform. They might have to wait days for a connection. There are some journeys that take nearly a week to complete. The platforms are full of activity. There are people selling cups of tea and stalls with hot and cold food. Shoeshine boys run up to passengers asking if they can clean their shoes.

The hustle and bustle of an Indian railway station.
▼

Pradip gave the children's cases to two porters in red jackets. They carried the cases on their heads. They all walked along platform six. Pradip stopped at each carriage to read the sheet of paper displayed on the side of the carriage. Eventually he stopped at one. 'This is it,' he declared. 'This is our carriage.'

▲
India has many large industries. The factories of Bombay produce goods which are sold all over the world.

These factories need power. This is supplied by electricity brought to Bombay by cables such as these.
▼

▲
Bombay attracts many people who come looking for work. Many families have to live in make shift housing in areas where they can find work.

Industry in India
Bombay is the trade centre of India. It is a very large city with a long history. The docks and airport are busy all year round. There is a very big film industry and the factories of Bombay produce more goods than most other cities. India sends its own satellites into space. It has some very modern industries and sells its products all round the world. Many of the latest taxis in London are fitted with engines made in India.

ON THE TRAIN

Daksa asked her uncle how he knew which was their carriage. Pradip looked surprised. 'Don't you have this system in England?' he said. 'Let me explain then. This morning I called at the station and booked three sleepers on the 01.00 train. The railway clerks type, on to a sheet of paper, the names of all the passengers who book. They stick the sheets on the outside of the carriage. Look, your names are on this sheet.' Daksa and Arun read the list of names, which was typed in English.

PATEL Pradip:	Berth No 6
PATEL Daksa:	Berth No 7
PATEL Arun:	Berth No 8

Daksa climbed on to the top berth. The guard came round and gave all the passengers a blanket. Next an attendant asked if anyone wanted to order a meal. Pradip told him no as they had all eaten.

DAKSA   Is there a buffet car?

PRADIP   No. The attendant takes orders here. They are then phoned ahead to the next station and loaded on to the train freshly cooked. The attendant delivers the meal to you in your seat.

Arun thought all of this was great fun. Tea and sweet-sellers kept coming to the window trying to sell to the passengers. At exactly one o'clock the train pulled out. Indian trains are usually on time. They are a very reliable way to travel. Pradip and the children slept as the train travelled north. It was light when they reached Baroda.

Baroda Railway Station. More Indians use bicyces than use cars. The station car park at Baroda holds thousands of bikes. The water-seller charges 25 paise (about 2p) a glass.

◀ Pradip and the children rode through Baroda on a tonga. The roads are very busy.

Hindus regard the cow as sacred. Cows are cared for at many Hindu temples.
▼

Every city has a large number of temples, both old and new.
▼

The station there was smaller than at Bombay, but still busy. Outside, the station car park was full of bicycles. There were also taxis, autorickshaws and tongas waiting to pick up passengers. Autorickshaws are three-wheeled carriages with lambretta engines, and tongas are horse-drawn carriages. There was also a water-seller outside. The children asked Pradip if they could have a drink of water from the water-seller. Pradip would not let them in case the water was impure. The last thing Pradip wanted was for the two of them to be ill. The children asked if they could travel in a tonga. Pradip agreed and they set off on the road to his house.

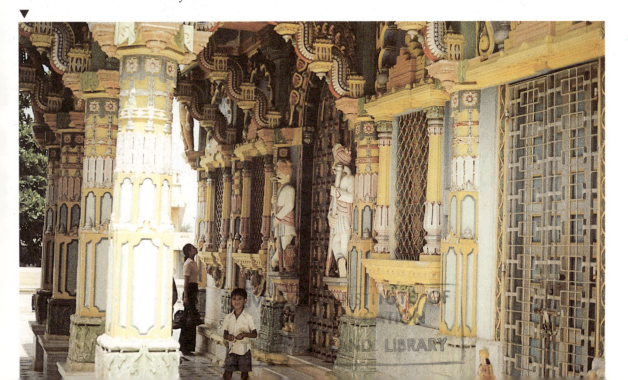

BARODA

The tonga drove down the main street in Baroda. The children passed the university, the shopping areas and the artificial lake. Arun was changing his mind about India. It was nothing like he had expected. They passed a magnificent building standing in large grounds. Pradip told them it was the palace of the Maharajah of Baroda. He also pointed out the new planetarium that had been built near the Palace.

Pradip lives on a new housing estate on the edge of the city. He was the engineer in charge of building the estate and he built the best house for his own family. Pradip's wife Kapila was standing at the door. She was wearing a sari and had a red mark on her forehead. The mark simply means that she is a married woman. Standing with Kapila were two girls and two boys.

Daksa was surprised. She knew that Pradip and Kapila had only two daughters. They were Silpa, aged thirteen, who was wearing a colourful dress and Minala, aged eleven, who was in a cotton skirt and T-shirt.

▲
In a hot country like India many of the day's lessons can be held in the fresh air. This is a science lesson for girls at secondary school.

▲
Children in class at a primary school. They write on boards which can be wiped clean and used again.

A nutrition educator explains to a group of village women how green leafy vegetables, like the ones she is holding in her hand, can prevent vitamin A deficiency.

DAKSA   Who are the boys?

PRADIP   They are your Uncle Ish's sons. The boy in the white shirt and cream trousers is Madhu. He's sixteen. The younger one is Nimla and he's eight. Ish still lives on the farm in the village. But in Gujarat the city schools are better than the village schools, so in term-time the boys come to Baroda and live with me. During the school holidays they go back to the village. My daughters go with them. That way they all learn about village life and town life.

Let's go in and you can meet them, and I'll get you a drink.

ARUN   Thanks, Uncle ... and when are we going to eat? I'm starving!

Daksa and Arun were taken to their rooms while Kapila prepared a meal. Only Madhu could speak any English so the children spoke in Gujarati.

Discussion points

In Britain most people live in towns and cities. In India most people live in villages. Imagine you were leaving your town to live in a British village. Make a list of the differences it would make to you. What would you enjoy about life in a village? What would you miss from the town? Here are some words to help you:

swimming pools	video shops
vandals	travel to school
petrol fumes	buses
friends nearby	places to play

Would you like to spend your term-time in the town and your holidays on a farm, like the children in Baroda?

Kapila smiled as she ate her meal. This was the first time she had eaten with her husband.

Kapila prepared a meal. Her daughters helped her in the kitchen. All three are very strict vegetarians. Arun asked if he could have an egg, but his aunt said no. Not only would she not eat anything that might contain life, but she would not cook it either. Kapila brought the food to the table and Pradip called to Arun.

PRADIP   Come on, Arun, we're going to eat now.

DAKSA   What about me?

PRADIP   In Gujarat, Daksa, the men eat first and when they have finished the women eat.

DAKSA   But I'm as hungry as Arun!

Pradip was in charge of building this housing estate in Baroda. The houses all have shower rooms, cool tile floors and flat roofs.

▲
The children enjoyed their visit to this well-kept park.

Doctor Joshi has his surgery near to Pradip's house. In India the doctor examines the patient and then supplies the medicine.

▶

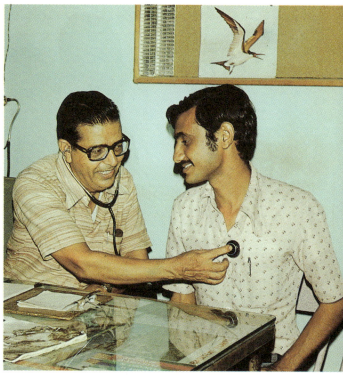

Daksa was used to eating last when she attended weddings and special festival meals. She was not used to eating last at home. Pradip realised this. 'Today,' he said, 'we shall all eat together. It is a special day. We have our guests from Britain.' Kapila could not stop smiling. Daksa wondered if she was doing something wrong. Kapila explained that she was laughing because she had never eaten with her husband before.

Kapila had put knives, forks and spoons on the table. Daksa realised that the cutlery was not normally used. 'You don't need to put the cutlery out, Aunt Kapila,' she said, 'We sometimes eat with our right hand at home. We can manage without knives and forks.'

The meal was served on stainless steel trays. There were various vegetables, many highly spiced. Chutneys, preserves, fresh salad and yoghurt were all available in the centre of the table. There was also a pile of chapattis which were useful for soaking up the juices left in the dish. Chapattis are a kind of bread made from flour, but they do not rise in the way British bread does because they are made without yeast.

There was plenty of ice-cold water from the fridge and a selection of fresh fruit. Pradip insisted that the children try a mango. He showed Daksa and Arun how to peel them, then he sliced them like peaches. The children both told him how much they enjoyed them. They did not tell him that their parents sold mangoes in their shop. To finish off the meal Silpa took some bottles of cola from the fridge. In India you cannot buy Coca Cola or Pepsi but you can buy a similar drink which is made in India. It tastes good and costs two rupees (about 10p) a bottle.

21

PRADIP'S HOUSE

Pradip's house is two storeys high. The weather in Gujarat can be very hot. To keep the house cool the floors are all tiled and there is an electric fan fitted to every ceiling. The house has a flat roof. When it is very warm the family take their mattresses on to the roof and sleep in the open air.

Daksa found Pradip's house more comfortable even than her own house in Britain. She was surprised to see a modern television set in the lounge. Indian television broadcasts for a few hours each day. The most popular programmes are cricket matches and Indian movies. Daksa realised that she was lucky having an uncle like Pradip. He was a very successful engineer and the richest of all her dad's relatives in India.

Daksa heard Arun calling her. 'Look, Daksa. Look at the sun!' Daksa rushed to the window. It was evening and the sun was a warm orange colour. It seemed to fall from the sky and vanish below the horizon. In Britain you see long, slow sunsets but in India there is a sudden change from day to night.

Daksa and Arun had been on the go for forty-eight hours. Kapila insisted they take a shower before going to bed. Like most Indians, the Patels prefer a shower to a bath. The toilet at their uncle's house is different from the type the children use at home. In Britain Daksa's family have the usual pedestal toilet which you sit on. Pradip's toilet was like those you sometimes find in France, Italy and other warm countries. There is a platform for the feet but nothing to sit on. Arun took a few days to get used to it. Daksa found it easier. Some of her Hindu friends had had them fitted in their homes in Preston, so she had used them before.

Hindu children often read the traditional stories of their gods in comics. The comics are printed in many languages including English.

Asian toilets do not have seats. It is usual to wash yourself with water rather than use toilet paper.

Things to do
Look at the rainfall chart for Gujarat.
In which months would it be foolish to sleep on the roof?
When could you sleep outside and be sure of waking up dry?
If there is flooding in Gujarat, when will it take place?

This chart shows the average monthly rainfall in Gujarat.

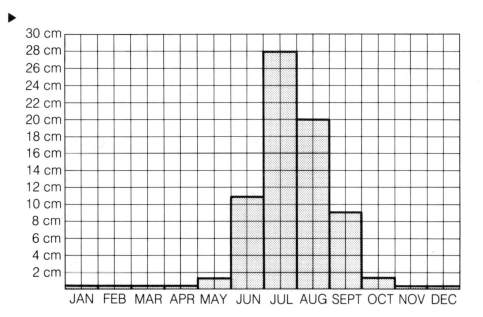

Navaratri

People everywhere have times of the year when they come together to enjoy themselves. In Gujarat a great autumn festival is held. It goes on for nine nights and is known as Navaratri, which literally means 'nine nights'.

Each of these nine nights is dedicated to different aspects of the goddess Durga. Statues and pictures of Durga show her with ten arms holding different weapons and riding on a tiger or a lion. Although Durga looks fierce she is also worshipped as a mother goddess. Many worshippers pray to different images of the mother goddess, to Parvati and to Amba. The mother goddess triumphs over evil and deserves respect. During Navaratri respect and love is shown for all mothers by Hindus.

The festival is celebrated all over India, but it is particularly colourful in Gujarat. It is a happy occasion with a lot of singing and dancing. Traditional Gujarati stick-dancing is performed and every evening the women do a special dance called **garba**. They move round and round a lamp singing and clapping their hands.

Navaratri is a time for music and dance. Singers and musicians play for nine nights. ▶

The crowds begin to gather at about nine o'clock. Everyone comes to watch the celebrations. ▶

The girls dance anti-clockwise around a circle.
They wear their best saris and a lot of jewellery.

All around the city large tableaux have been built.
Some statues of the Mother Goddess are bigger
than people.

▼

The children knew all about Navaratri. Gujaratis celebrate it in
Britain. It is a time for remembering all the things mothers do for the
family. Young married women try to visit their mothers during this
festival. In Britain the statue of the Mother Goddess is at the centre of
the celebrations. The children wondered if it would be the same in
India.

There are open spaces in the middle of the new housing estates in
Baroda. The one near Pradip's house was decorated with flags and
coloured lights. A stage had been erected and a microphone wired up
to speakers. At about nine o'clock the children heard music playing
over the loudspeakers. Kapila and her daughters were dressed in their
finest saris. Even the youngest girls had eye-shadow to match their
saris. Daksa was wearing jeans and a blouse. She had forgotten to
pack a sari. All the boys wore clean clothes, but it was clear to Arun
that Navaratri was a time when the girls had all the attention.

By the time they reached the clearing there were hundreds of people
sitting around the edge. In the centre a group played and sang.
Women and girls of all ages danced anti-clockwise around the singers.
They clapped their hands and sang as they moved to the music. The
whole thing was spectacular. The boys stood and watched.

ARUN   At home the boys join in. Why don't you?

MADHU   We did until last year, but some of the girls complained we were too
        rough, so this year we have to watch. Don't worry though, we'll join
        in later when the grown-ups go to bed.

Madhu and the others took Arun around the town. Every district
had its own dance area. In some parts of Baroda there were enormous
statues of the Mother Goddess.

▲ Most statues are made of clay. These people spend all year making and painting statues which will be needed for the celebrations.

▶

Thousands of people filled the streets. They were visiting the various clearings to see the dancers. Uncle Pradip and his friends were standing by a peanut-seller's stall. He bought all the boys some nuts and sweets.

The boys arrived back at their own estate at about one o'clock. Many of the older people had gone home to bed. The young men now joined in the dancing. At two o'clock in the morning the whole celebration ended with **arti**, when religious songs were sung and food offered to the Mother Goddess.

Everyone went straight to bed. Arun had enjoyed himself, but Daksa was upset. She had wanted to dance, but felt out of place in her jeans. She was the last to go to sleep as peace and quiet gradually returned to Baroda.

Daksa was woken next day by Kapila shaking her. 'Come on Daksa. The autorickshaw is waiting outside. I want you to come shopping with me.' They drove into town and walked up and down past the shops until Kapila saw a sari she liked. Daksa and Kapila entered the shop. It was not like any shop Daksa had been in before. The floor was covered with an enormous mattress. Kapila took off her sandals and sat in the middle of the mattress. Daksa did the same.

The shopkeeper asked what he could do for them and Kapila said she wanted a sari for Daksa. Daksa could not believe her ears. Kapila had realised how she felt and was making sure that she would not miss another night's celebrations. Kapila insisted on American quality for the sari, which is the best quality. The shopkeeper produced sari after sari until Daksa decided on a beautiful red one. It had gold embroidery and shimmered as she moved. Kapila paid him and they left the shop to return home.

That night there was one more dancer in the Navaratri celebrations and even Arun had to admit that nobody looked better than Daksa.

◄ Daksa was really upset. She felt the odd one out in her jeans.

Kapila knew how Daksa was feeling. She took her to buy a new sari so that she could join in the dancing.
▼

THE WEDDING

It was the day of cousin Amita's wedding. Amita had been born in Britain but had moved to India at the age of eighteen. The marriage had been arranged by Amita's parents and the parents of the groom.

Guests began arriving early in the morning. There are usually hundreds of people at a Hindu wedding and the festivities can go on for days. The wedding took place in a large courtyard. In the centre of the courtyard there were two silver seats covered by a canopy. This area is regarded as sacred and it is here that the priest conducts the marriage ceremony.

The groom arrived first. He was dressed in a blue suit. Daksa had expected him to wear something Indian. In fact he looked just like a bridegroom in Britain. A garland was placed round his neck. The bride came next, dressed in a magnificent wedding sari. A Hindu bride always wears a red and gold sari at her wedding. Her face and hands were decorated with a red vegetable dye called henna and she wore gold jewellery.

The Hindu wedding ritual takes hours to complete. A fire, which is a sign of purity, always burns while the priest conducts the ceremony. The priest chants in Sanskrit, the ancient language of India, and many offerings of coconut, flowers, leaves, sweetmeats, ghee (clarified butter), rice and other things are made. Guests come and go during the ceremony, sometimes watching, sometimes walking around and sometimes talking to other guests. The ceremony ended in the late afternoon. Afterwards a meal was served. The guests ate their food off large palm leaves used as plates. No alcohol was drunk.

A fire always burns at a Hindu wedding as a sign of purity.
▼

▲
The bridegroom wore a dark blue suit, shirt and tie.

28

The priest sits with the bride and groom. The wedding ceremony takes hours to complete.

The following day Daksa was taken to another ceremony at a friend's house. Two young couples had recently been married. Before they moved into their new homes a service was being held for them. A priest came along and laid out a small fire, ghee lamps and many offerings, all in silver containers. He blessed the newly married couples and prayed that they would be happy in the future. Many Hindu families pay a priest to say special prayers on important occasions in their lives. Business people pay him to come and pray for a good year's business on New Year's Eve.

The family priest visits the house to perform a ceremony. These people have recently married and the priest blesses them. All the guests share in the meal.

CASTE

Daksa talked to her Aunt Kapila about the marriage.

DAKSA Why don't Hindu parents let their children fall in love and marry whoever they like? Most of my schoolfriends in Britain will just meet boys and marry them.

KAPILA When you were small your mum and dad used to stop you running across the road.

DAKSA What's that got to do with getting married?

KAPILA They stopped you running across the road because they knew more about roads than you. Adults have experience of life. Parents arrange weddings because they want to be sure the person you marry is good, kind and trustworthy. We always arrange weddings between people of the same caste as ourselves. The members of our caste all come originally from thirty villages around Gujarat. When people leave those villages they are still part of our caste. Even if they go to live in the USA, Canada, Britain or in the cities of India. When it is time to marry they choose someone from their own caste.

> ## Caste
> Hindu society was traditionally divided into **castes** according to trade or craft. These groups of people are related by marriage or descended from the same ancestors. They help one another, share the same customs and often work together.
>
> All members of a caste have the same surname and there are many castes with the same name. People usually marry within their own caste, particularly in the villages of India.

▲
There are many statues carved from stone in the temples, like this one of Ganesh.

Pradip wanted to take the children to the temple which the Patel family attended. Arun was surprised to find it was not like the temple at home. In Britain the Hindu temples are also meeting places. The people join together for prayers and worship. In India many of the temples do not have large rooms. They have many small rooms and narrow passageways. The worshipper prays and worships alone. The other difference noticed by the children was the statues. In Britain the statues of the gods are kept in the temples. In India there are statues outside and on the walls as well as inside. Many of the statues are carved from stone.

The temple Pradip showed them had some very steep steps. Aunt Kapila explained that as they climb the steps, worshippers feel as though they are approaching nearer to their god.

Lakshmi, the goddess of wealth, and Ganesh, the remover of obstacles. In Britain many of the small statues of gods are made out of plastic. The children saw some plastic gods on sale in the city but not in the village.

Many people in the village pray at this ▶ small shrine.

Things to do

All the members of a caste have the same surname, but this does not mean they all do the same work. Not all Patels are farmers, just as in Britain people with the name Carpenter have many different jobs. Surnames give us clues about the past. They can help us trace our family history. Can you find the meaning of your own surname?

Check the meanings of the names of the others in your class. Try to divide them into groups, such as the following:

1   Names that tell us about jobs, for example Patel, Smith and Carpenter.
2   Names that tell us about the places our ancestors came from, for example Bolton, Scott and French.
3   Names with clues at the end of the name, for example Rob*son*, Harri*son* and Ghari*wallah*.
4   Names with the clue at the beginning, for example *Mac*millan, *Fitz*gerald and *O*'Hara.

VILLAGE LIFE

It was time for Arun and Daksa to leave Baroda. Their next stop was the village where their father had been born.

In Britain many families own a car. In India it is very different. There are fewer cars. Only people with very good jobs can afford one. The children had seen many cars in Bombay, but most of these are taken there by foreigners. In most of India there are only two models available — a Fiat and an Austin. Both types are made in India, and they both look old-fashioned. Pradip owns a Fiat. He drove the children along the main road in the direction of the village. As they travelled they saw monkeys in the trees.

ARUN   Where are the elephants, Uncle? I've seen pictures at school of elephants working in India.

PRADIP   You're forgetting how big India is. Think of it as a continent. There are working elephants in South India. The only ones in the north are in zoos, or used to carry tourists.

After about fifty kilometres Pradip turned off the main road onto a sandy track. In the rainy season it is impossible to drive on these roads. They passed two villages. Pradip explained that one of them was a Muslim village. There are many Muslims in Gujarat. Hindu and Muslim villages are often close together and the people are friendly towards each other.

Pradip stopped the car just outside the village. In no time they were surrounded by children. It was like a procession as Pradip led Daksa

▲
Charu sat in front of the cot with her daughter Jyoti beside her and baby Dipak on her lap.

▲
Dipak and Jyoti were quiet at first. Jyoti had never met her cousins from Britain before.

The Patel family live in a comfortable house with running water and electricity.

and Arun to their grandad's house. The first thing they saw as they entered the house was their Aunt Charu, Ish's wife, with Dipak, her tiny son and her daughter, Jyoti. The cot in which Dipak slept was beautifully carved and decorated with a red design.

Grandad stood up. He put his hands together and bowed to Pradip and the children. They did the same and spoke the usual Hindu greeting, 'Namaste'.

The poor people live in much smaller houses. Light is provided by oil lamps and they have to walk to the village well for their water.

Grandma brought them sweets and a drink. Pradip introduced everyone including Ish, their uncle. Ish was the brother who had stayed in the village to help grandad on the farm. Ish took the children out to look around the village.

As they walked Daksa realised the village was in two parts. In the centre of the village there was a pond. On one side of the pond stood houses built of brick. Most of these were two or three storeys high. On the other side the houses were smaller and made of clay. The children visited more than a dozen homes, including two on the poor side of the village.

Arun knew all about the Indian custom of giving food and drink to visitors, but he had not expected to visit so many homes. Unfortunately he helped himself to large portions of food and by the time he visited the sixth house he looked quite ill. Ish told him it served him right for being greedy. Even so, Arun had to eat a little at all the other houses. It is bad manners to refuse.

As they visited the villagers' homes, Daksa began to notice great differences. The brick houses had piped water and electricity. Their floors were tiled and they had good furniture. The clay houses had oil lamps. There was no water supply for them. Arun saw women from these homes walking to the well to collect water in buckets. Their homes had very little furniture. The people who lived in these houses were the poorest Arun had seen since he arrived in India. Even so they looked fit and strong.

ARUN   Uncle Ish, in Britain we keep hearing about people in India starving. Does anyone around here die from hunger?

ISH   There are parts of India which are very poor. In some areas the rain does not always fall. In other districts the soil is thin and floods wash it away. In this part of Gujarat we are lucky. We have not suffered much from drought, although there are parts of Gujarat which do flood. But mostly it is a good place to live. You will not see starving people in this village, Arun.

The labourers live in small homes. Tools and shoes are hung from the ceiling because there is little storage space.

The village does not have its own doctor. A visiting doctor calls regularly to check that the villagers are in good health.

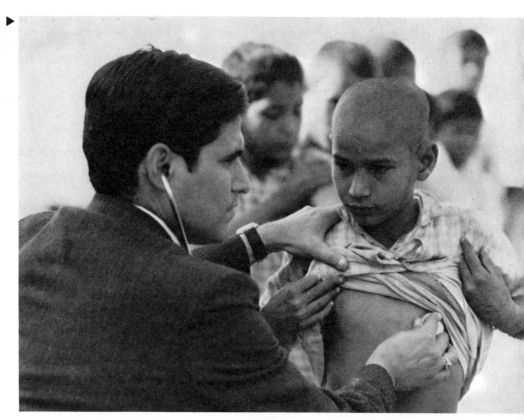

Some villagers leave the village because there is no work for them on the land. They travel to the big cities and live in makeshift homes like this.

The carpenter works in his house. His son is learning to be a carpenter by watching his father at work.

Daksa was still thrilled with the beauty of Dipak's cot. Pradip took her to visit the carpenter who had made it. The carpenter lived about a hundred metres from Ish's home. His workshop was the main room of his house. Pradip explained that the carpenter supplied the whole village. He made everything from wooden spoons to staircases.

Pradip also pointed to the carpenter's son. He said that one day the boy would follow his father as the village carpenter.

When the weather is fine, food is cooked outside in the courtyard. Only in bad weather is the indoor oven used.

DAKSA   How do you know that Uncle? Perhaps he will want to be a farmer or something else.

PRADIP   I don't think so Daksa. In Hindu villages the people belong to different castes. It might be a farmer caste or a carpenter caste or a washerman, fisherman or labourer caste. You and Arun were born into a caste, too.

ARUN   But when I grow up I don't have to be a shopkeeper like dad. I might be an engineer or a teacher.

PRADIP   You are right, Arun. Once people leave the village to live in cities they can choose. Village life is different from city life. We have always followed the rules of caste here. Patels will always be farmers, the children of cowherds will become cowherds and the carpenter's son will be the carpenter one day.

Daksa's relatives lived in the big houses. They were the landowners. Those in the small houses were labourers who had no land.

They returned to Ish's for the evening meal. This time the men all sat down to eat first. Daksa was expected to help her grandma prepare the food. Everyone in the village was a strict vegetarian. Uncle Ish would never think of eating a chicken dinner or drinking alcohol. Daksa realised that the two brothers who had left the village had changed a great deal.

The meal took a long time to prepare. All the vegetables, sauces and spices are prepared in different pans and served in different dishes. Daksa dreaded the washing-up, but Charu told her not to worry about it. 'We have a woman from the other side of the village who comes here each day,' she told Daksa. 'She washes our clothes in the morning. In the evening she cleans the pans. Your aunt in Baroda has a woman who does the same jobs. Perhaps you didn't notice her. She walks into Baroda each day from her village. She works at Kapila's house. She goes home just before dark.'

The meal is cooked and served in many pans and dishes. The pile of dirty pots seemed enormous to Daksa.

▼

In the villages Hindu men do not normally shave themselves. Every day they visit the village barber who gives them a close-shave.   ▶

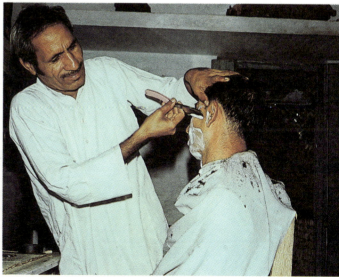

After they had eaten, the children were shown around the house. There was a tiled floor and a ceiling fan. The house had a telephone and a radio/cassette player. The radio was covered to keep it cool. There were three chairs and a swing to sit on. It was like a wide garden swing for four people. They went upstairs. Arun asked why the stairs were covered in dry mud.

ISH   It isn't mud Arun. It's dried cow dung.

ARUN   What! I'm walking on cow dung! Ugh, why didn't you tell me?

ISH   You've been in and out of houses all day. All those mud floors were cow dung. You couldn't tell because once it has baked dry there is no smell. Now you're pulling a face. You're a real city boy, Arun. We use the dung because it keeps the house cool in summer and warm in winter.

DAKSA   Do you know, Uncle, I've been on school trips at home in Britain. We visited some houses which the teacher said were made of wattle and daub mixed with cow dung. So people must always have used it.

ISH   We use it because it's cheap. We can't pay high prices for materials from the city. Farming people learn to use whatever is near at hand.

It took Arun some time to get used to the idea. He sat on his bed for ten minutes with his feet off the ground. Finally he realised that he had better get used to it. He could not stay on his bed for the next four weeks.

The woman who cleans for Charu also does some of the shopping. The shopkeeper sells loose food. It is weighed in front of the customer.

▲
Dung is very valuable. It is used on the land as a
fertiliser and in houses on the walls and floors. It
can also be dried and used for fuel. This dung has
been pressed into small cakes and is drying in the
sun. Then it will be burned as fuel for boiling water.

Out in the fields the women pick cotton. As long as ▶
the cotton is picked by hand there will be jobs on
the land.

Cows

The cow is regarded as a sacred animal by Hindus. Cows are
protected by the law; harming one is a serious offence.

The products of the cow are all considered to be very pure. Milk
and yoghurt are important ingredients of diet in India, as is ghee.
Ghee is made from melted butter by skimming off the solid fat,
leaving only the liquid butter. It keeps for a very long time, even in a
hot climate.

Discussion point

We often think that whatever we do is 'normal' and that whatever others
do is 'strange'. Some British people think it is strange that snails and
frogs' legs are eaten in France. People from India often find it strange
when they see British people being licked on the face by their dogs.

Are there any things you do that your family does not like? Ask your
friends about their 'hates'. Are they the same as yours?

DASSEHRA

That night Arun and Daksa walked to the village square to watch the Navaratri celebrations. The music was provided by the men while the women danced. The saris of the villagers were not as expensive as those worn in Baroda. Even so, there was great colour and excitement as the celebrations went on until midnight.

Everyone was awake and dressed by six o'clock the next day for the festival of Dassehra. The barber called at Ish's house to shave all the men. Hindu men in the villages do not usually shave themselves.

Dassehra
Dassehra means 'tenth'. This festival is on the tenth day after Navaratri begins. On this day Hindus celebrate Rama's victory over the demon king Ravana, who had stolen Rama's wife, Sita. The goddess Durga had helped Rama defeat Ravana. The story of Rama and Sita is one of the best known and favourite Hindu tales. At the end of the festival huge images of Ravana and his accomplices are set alight and burnt.

Young women carry the plants to the village pond. They are followed by friends and relatives.
▼

In the villages the celebration of Dassehra is like a harvest festival. Plants are grown in most homes and temples and there is singing and dancing around them.

At a quarter to eight in the morning the first of these plants are brought into the streets. They are placed on boards and carried on the

▲
A long procession
winds its way through
the village to the
pond.

heads of young women. They are blessed at the shrines and temples in
the village. More and more women appear carrying plants and they
are followed in each street by all those who live nearby. Soon a great
procession threads its way towards the village pond. It is led by a man
playing tabla (drums) and another playing a harmonium.

The crowds sing and chant. Some people become so excited that
they fall on the ground in a trance. The procession reaches the village
pond but the young women do not go any further. Instead, the plants
are passed to the young men who carry them down into the water. All
the men line up, side by side. They bend their knees and disappear
beneath the water. A few moments later the men appear again, but the
plants have gone forever.

The plants are
passed to young men
who carry them into
the village pond
where they are sunk. ▶

VARANASI

The festival was over. Ish explained to Arun and Daksa that Hindus often end their ceremonies with the gods returning to the water. The festival was like life. A plant germinates, grows, ripens and then dies. So it is with people. We are born, we grow, we live on this earth but then we die. To the Hindu, death is not the end. At death the soul leaves the body and it returns to a different body to begin another existence.

Daksa remembered what her teacher at school had told her about harvest in Britain. Villagers used to 'kill' the last of the corn. They believed that the Corn Goddess had to die so she could return with a new harvest the next year. Many people still make corn dollies which represent the Corn Goddess.

Pradip, Kapila and the children travelled from Ahmadabad to Varanasi via Delhi.

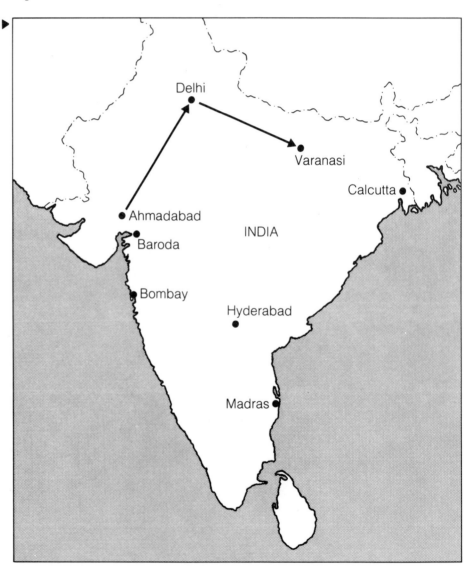

Indian life cycle ►

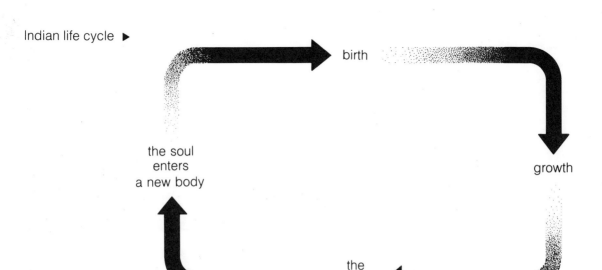

The children's time in the village was coming to an end. Daksa and Arun had grown to like the people there. Their relatives were pleased the children had come, and asked them to persuade the whole family to come and visit. Daksa and Arun realised that everyone in the village expected their parents to return to live there one day. Arun wanted to tell them that he knew his mum and dad would never come back. Daksa told him not to say so. The children knew that their parents were settled in Britain. They could never return to live in the village. But Daksa was sure it would upset the relatives if they were told that Narendra would never live there again, so she said nothing.

Pradip and Kapila came to collect Daksa and Arun. Their luggage was loaded into Pradip's car and the two children said their last goodbyes. The whole village seemed to be there to see them off.

Before going back to Baroda, Pradip and Kapila were taking the children to visit the city of Varanasi, or Benares as it is called by the British. They drove to the city of Ahmadabad, where they would continue their journey by plane. As they travelled across the city they saw great images of Ravana burning. Pradip told them that in some parts of the city, workers burn models of their boss instead of the demon king!

They were soon at Ahmadabad airport. Their flight took them to New Delhi, the capital of India, and from there on to Varanasi. It is the holiest city of the Hindus and is an important pilgrimage centre. All Hindus try to visit Varanasi at least once. It is situated on the banks of the sacred river Ganges. Many Hindus go there if they are ill or suffering.

Uncle Pradip, Aunt Kapila, Daksa and Arun were tired when they reached their modern hotel near the city centre. All four of them ate some supper and went straight to bed. They would not sleep for long. In Varanasi people have to be up early if they want to see daybreak over the Ganges.

▲ At dawn pilgrims begin to gather on the west bank of the River Ganges.

Pilgrims dip their whole body in the river and sip a little river water. ►

There are many religious teachers in Varanasi who are visited by the pilgrims.
▼

The phone rang in the children's room to tell them it was five o'clock. They dressed quickly and hurried downstairs where Pradip and Kapila were waiting for them. As they walked towards the centre of Varanasi Arun asked them all to stop and listen. The tinkling of small handbells could be heard from all directions. The early morning prayers had begun.

They hurried on towards the river. The streets were already busy with pilgrims. The nearer they moved to the river the narrower the streets became. Pradip and Kapila held the children's hands. It would be easy to lose each other in the crush. They walked to the end of a narrow passage and suddenly they were in the open again. All four just stood and looked down the great stone steps to the river below.

Beyond the opposite bank dawn was breaking. Pilgrims lined the west banks facing towards the east, ready to glimpse the first rays of the sun.

Large amounts of wood are available for the cremation of the dead.

Pradip led the children and Kapila down the steps to the River Ganges. They boarded a boat just as the sun appeared above the horizon. The boat was full of visitors who had come to watch the pilgrims. They sailed into the middle of the river. The children could now see the full range of activity that was taking place. Bells were ringing, conch shells were being blown. Some Hindus prayed whilst others walked down the steps to bathe in the waters of the Ganges. Religious teachers spoke to pilgrims about the way they ought to live. The scene was full of life and colour.

The boat sailed along for a while until it drew level with the ghats (stone banks) where the bodies of dead Hindus are cremated. The bodies are brought to the pyre wrapped in cloth. The appropriate amount of wood is weighed and placed on the ghat. The eldest son of the dead person lights the funeral pyre and the body is burned. The ashes of the dead are thrown onto the river. The cycle of life has ended.

The children returned to the river bank at about nine o'clock and made their way back to the hotel. Their visit to Varanasi and the Ganges was one they would never forget. The following day they too bathed in the Ganges as Hindu pilgrims have done for so many years.

The bodies of the dead are brought to these stone steps (ghats) by relatives. After cremation the ashes are scattered on the river.

DIWALI

Arun and Daksa returned to Baroda with Pradip and Kapila. They were booked on a flight from Bombay to England on 5 November. Before they left Gujarat they took part in one more important event, the festival of Diwali.

Diwali

Diwali is the festival of lights. Every house is lit up with diwas (oil lamps) to show Rama the way home after his period of exile. The festival is also dedicated to Lakshmi, the goddess of wealth and prosperity.

The date of this festival follows a calendar which is different from the calendar we use in Britain. It can occur in October or November, and lasts five days. In Gujarat, Diwali is also a New Year festival. The year begins on the first day of Diwali. In some parts of India another calendar is used and the year begins in March or April.

Diwali is the beginning of the year in many parts of India. Friends and relatives send each other Diwali cards like these.

Every house in Baroda was lit up. There were candles, lanterns and fairy lights. Some were strung across the streets. The great temples in the city were covered with coloured lights. One temple had a giant notice board which was like a scoreboard at a football ground. It flashed up 'Happy New Year' in both Gujarati and English.

On the night before the festival began the shops were open until late. Every shop window had a sales notice displayed. People hurried to and fro buying last-minute presents and cards. Daksa thought it was just like the New Year Sales in Britain. All the streets echoed with the sound of fireworks. Arun was surprised that so many people were still working. He heard the rattle of looms as the cloth workers continued to work late into the night.

Pradip took the children to a temple in the town centre. At the temple a special puja (worship) for Diwali was taking place. There were so many people there, it was impossible to move. Celebrations continued after the puja all through the night. Arun was woken the next day by more fireworks being set off. He looked at his watch and was amazed to find it was only five o'clock. New Year's Day had certainly started with a bang!

It was time for Daksa and Arun to return to Britain. Their stay in India had been a wonderful experience, but they were homesick. Arun had begun to miss his favourite television programmes, his comics and his friends. Daksa had had enough of the heat and dust. Although she had visited India at the best time of the year, she still found it hot during the day. Both of them knew that India was special to them. This had been their first visit but it would not be their last.

Daksa felt she could probably live in an Indian city but not in a village. She liked the bustle of city life. Arun simply talked about the one thing he was going to do when he reached Britain. It was something he had not done since he arrived in India. He wanted to eat a bag of chips!

Some people, such as these dairy workers, keep working even at Diwali. Milk must still be delivered to the people in the city.

▼

TEACHER'S NOTES

The *At Home and Abroad* series is designed to start from what the child knows — Britain — and to move to the distant location. It is intended that the characters in the books are seen as brown/black British rather than the increasingly anachronistic 'immigrant'.

The text aims to introduce a number of key concepts. The table below lists the main ones but is not exhaustive.

Page

Page	Concepts
4/5	Change; cause/consequence
6/7	Distance
8/9	Adaptation
10/11	Tradition; social change
12/13	Similarity/difference
14/15	Values/beliefs
16/17	Similarity/difference
18/19	Similarity/difference
20/21	Tradition; values/beliefs; sex roles
22/23	Cause/effect; location
24/25	Tradition
26/27	Values/beliefs; sex roles
28/29	Similarity/difference; Tradition
30/31	Sex roles; values/beliefs; tradition
32/33	Change; location
34/35	Tradition; interdependence
36/37	Similarity/difference; tradition; social change
38/39	Interdependence; power
40/41	Values/beliefs
42/43	Similarity/difference; tradition
44/45	Values/beliefs
46/47	Change; adaptation

The books are also intended to provide a vehicle for teachers to encourage pupils in the exploration of values and attitudes. It is hoped that these will include open-mindedness, evaluation, empathy, curiosity, exploration of attitudes and openness to change, an interest in human affairs, willingness to look for causes and tolerance for the belief systems of others.